FEARLESS AND FAITHFUL

D1334078

FEARLESS AND FAITHFUL

LINDA FINLAYSON

CF4·K

For my nieces
Nicola, Katya, Christina,
Catriona, Kendra, Andrea,
Ginevra, Caroline, Larissa,
Emily, Sarah.

10 9 8 7 6 5 4 3 2 1
© Copyright 2010 Linda Finlayson
Christian Focus Publications
ISBN: 978-1-84550-588-2

Published by Christian Focus Publications,
Geanies House, Fearn, Tain, Ross-shire,
IV20 1TW, Scotland, U.K.
www.christianfocus.com
E-mail:info@christianfocus.com

Cover design by Daniel van Straaten
Cover illustration by Neil Reed

Character and chapter illustrations by Neil Reed
Maps by Fred Apps
Printed and bound by Norhaven AS, Denmark

CONTENTS

LET'S GET STARTED

Risks are all around us. In everyday life we take risks with most things we do. We could slip in the bath, find ourselves in a car crash or eat food in a restaurant that wasn't properly prepared. All of those things would be called accidents. They certainly aren't planned events.

Athletes take risks as they train for their sport. Snowboarders or skiers push themselves to try more and more difficult manoeuvres until they master them, but they don't do it foolishly. They work up to the more difficult things slowly, and they keep their bodies fit to be able to withstand the rigours of their sport.

None of these are 'a venture undertaken without regard to the possibility of suffering harm, loss or danger.' They are part of everyday living or part of preparation for a sport. A venture is more like taking a gamble or a risk, only thinking about what you can get in return for exposing yourself to unnecessary danger.

Maybe you've taken some silly risks without thinking about the danger. Something like accepting a dare to kiss a frog, even though it could make you ill. Or go swimming in a dangerous place just to prove you're brave. Those are foolish risks.

Maybe you know of someone who likes to try the more extreme sports or perform dangerous stunts. But they do them on the spur of the moment, rather than taking time to prepare properly for them. They take those risks, not because they want to excel at something, but because they like the thrill or adrenaline rush they get. When we are faced with a dangerous situation our bodies begin pumping adrenaline which gives a surge of energy and excitement. Some people like that feeling so much they do more and more dangerous things to keep the adrenaline pumping, and take no thought for safety. Very foolish indeed.

So when is it a good thing to take a risk? Learning new things always comes with a risk, like learning to drive a car. But you don't just start driving without having studied the rules of the road or having an instructor. Meeting new people can be risky because we don't know if they will be good friends or not. But these things are still good risks, especially because we do them carefully.

In this book we will learn about people who took good risks. They chose to take a risk, not for the thrill, not to prove something to anyone else, but to obey God. Jesus warned his disciples that following him was not an easy thing. Christians can expect to be persecuted, beaten, put in prison and even risk death. But for all of that risk, Jesus promised that he would be with his followers, giving them strength and courage, as well as a wonderful home in heaven. Now that's something worth taking a risk for, don't you think?

Come on an adventure now and read about heroines from long ago and in recent times who took such risks. Follow one woman as she challenges a king, another who bravely stands up to an angry tribal chief, someone who escapes an enemy by travelling through the mountains, another who is captured by a rebel lord, and finally two Bible characters who obeyed God and risked their lives for him. These are the kind of risks that God asked of those who loved him.

Are you that kind of person?

ELIZABETH WELCH

Elizabeth was the youngest daughter of John Knox, a fiery preacher who helped bring the Reformation to Scotland in the 1500's. She was born around 1570 and probably in Edinburgh. When Elizabeth grew up, she married a minister too, named John Welch. In 1603 Scottish King James VI also became King of England and became known as James I. King James issued decrees that everyone in Scotland and England should worship the same way. He wanted to keep the English style of worship and church government, which included priests and bishops. Those in Scotland, who thought the Bible told them to worship more simply without the need for great ceremony or bishops, said no to the king. John Welch, Elizabeth's husband, was one of those men.

In 1605 John Welch was arrested along with other ministers for defying the king's orders. He endured a year in prison in Blackness Castle near Edinburgh. After a year, the king decided to exile John Welch to France. Elizabeth joined her husband in his exile with their children and they lived there for sixteen years. John studied the French language so he could continue preaching, and he ministered in three different churches. In the last town they settled in, St. Jean D'Angely, they faced the French army who had besieged the town, but God protected them. So by the time Elizabeth had reached middle age, she had faced the difficulty of her husband's arrest and imprisonment, being exiled with him to France and the dangers of an invading army. Surely she had faced enough risks for God. But there was one more to come.

THE DANGEROUS DEBATE

(1622)

Elizabeth woke to the sound of birds singing and her husband coughing. The dawn light was breaking through the slats in the wooden shutters on the window by the bed. Leaning over to her husband, Elizabeth rubbed his back as he gasped for air after his coughing fit. Above her head she could hear their two youngest children, Louise and Nathaniel stirring in their loft beds. The two older boys had been sent back to Scotland for their education.

'I'll get you something to drink to ease your chest,' Elizabeth said as she reached over and handed him his plaid.

John nodded, still unable to speak. He pulled his plaid around his shoulders and started to cough again.

Elizabeth pulled her dark blue gown over her linen chemise and did up the buttons down the bodice front. Then she tied her full white apron over on top. She didn't take time to add a collar or cuffs or even her stockings. Pushing her feet into soft leather shoes, she walked around the bed toward the kitchen area at the other end of the stone cottage. She opened the spigot on the ale barrel and filled a mug. John sipped it gratefully as his coughing spell eased again.

Elizabeth was worried about her husband. He looked older than his fifty years. Ever since his imprisonment at Blackness Castle many years earlier, his health had not been strong. But now she was afraid that he was getting even worse. She sighed while she pinned her grey braid on top of her head and tied her white cap on top.

Nathaniel came down the loft ladder with a young man's clatter. He cheerfully greeted his parents before going to build up the fire in the stone hearth. Nine-year-old Louise arrived a few minutes later in a more dignified manner and began laying the table for the morning meal. She cast worried glances at her father as he shrugged his wide shoulders into his doublet and fastened it in front.

After they broke their fast, they remained at the wooden trestle table to begin their morning devotions. A knock sounded at the door and Nathaniel leapt up to answer it. Two men from the local Huguenot congregation entered. They were dressed soberly in dark coloured doublets and breeches. They removed their soft hats and bowed to both John and Elizabeth.

'Come in, *mes amis*,' John welcomed them and offered them seats on the bench at the table. 'Please join us for our Sabbath morning worship.'

'Thank you,' one of them replied. 'But we came only to persuade you to remain at home today. The doctor tells us your health is worsening, Mr. Welch. Please rest. Someone else can preach today.'

'Nonsense,' John replied. 'As long as God gives me breath, I must preach. I can do nothing else.'

Elizabeth said nothing. She understood her husband's call to be a minister, even in this foreign land. He had studied the French language carefully when they first arrived so he could preach God's Word to the French people. But she worried about his health.

The men shook their heads. 'Very well. If you are able, we do love to hear you speak of the things of God. We will see you later at worship.'

After they left, John patted Elizabeth's hand. 'I must serve God,' he said, knowing very well what she was thinking.

She smiled in return. 'Of course you must.'

Later that day John entered the pulpit in the small stone church and began to preach. The benches were filled with people eager to hear their fiery minister. No one slept when John Welch preached. But he didn't finish his sermon. He already spoke more slowly than he once did and he leaned on the pulpit for support. Then a coughing fit began and weakened him so much that he had to stop and be helped home. The congregation remained behind, praying for their ailing pastor.

The doctor came and shook his head at John as he lay in his bed. 'I told you that you must rest. But even that won't cure you, Mr. Welch. I believe that only if you breathe your native air in Scotland will you begin to feel better. Surely after all this time the English king will let you return.'

Elizabeth stood by the bed. 'The king is a stubborn man. It's not likely he will change his mind,' she said. And then she paused. 'Although I suppose we could always ask him.'

John smiled weakly, his face as pale as the sheet that covered him. 'I'm sure *you* could, my dear.'

And so it was decided. First they must write and ask permission to return to England to speak to the king. Surprisingly the king gave his permission, but only for them to come to London, and John was not allowed to preach. So then the preparation for the long journey from the south of France to London began.

Elizabeth packed up their belongings, giving away their household furniture and other items to needy people. They would travel lightly with only their clothes and John's books in a small box. They had a long journey ahead.

They arrived in London feeling just as much like foreigners there as they had felt in France. How both John and Elizabeth longed for Scotland, wishing that their journey was ending in Ayr and not in this noisy, dirty city. Making the best of it, they gratefully settled in the home of some fellow believers who had heard of their coming.

Letters from France had arrived more quickly than the Welch family. The letters told of John's poor health and of his hopes that King James would relent and allow him to return home to Scotland. Meanwhile, the Christians in London were anxious to meet this famous preacher for themselves. Many came to visit him in the Welch family lodgings, gathering around the wooden table, with Bibles open, discussing doctrines. Elizabeth understood, but was aware that even this exertion left her husband weak.

Meanwhile they waited. Elizabeth knew she couldn't just walk up to the front door of the palace and ask to see the king. She had to ask friends, who would ask their friends, who knew someone at the court, who could get permission for Elizabeth to come to the king's court. It all took time and as John seemed weaker each day, Elizabeth worried that she might not get to speak with the king at all.

At last the summons came. Elizabeth put on her best dress, a dark red gown with a wide lace collar and lace cuffs. She wore a matching lace trimmed white apron and cape. As she entered the corridors of the palace, she realised she was very plainly dressed. Both the men and women of the court wore clothing trimmed with furs, gold and silver braid, along with much jewellery. Ignoring their unfriendly stares she followed the steward to the door of the King's Presence Chamber. Taking a deep breath she entered the room full of people and saw the king himself standing at the far end.

Elizabeth marched up to the tall thin man richly dressed in gold trimmed doublet and breeches with a long fur lined open coat. She curtsied deeply to him and lightly kissed the hand he held out to her. Then she rose to her feet and heard people around her gasp. The king had not given her permission to rise. But Elizabeth didn't want to waste any more time. It had already taken too long to get here. She looked the middle-aged king in the eye.

He stared back at her, his bearded face grim.

'Who is your father?' the king suddenly demanded.

'John Knox,' Elizabeth replied proudly.

The king's eyes widened. 'You're Knox's daughter and Welch's wife? The devil couldn't have thought up a better match than that!'

'We certainly never asked his advice!' Elizabeth shot back.

The king had more questions and Elizabeth felt as if she were on trial. She was aware that the room was now silent, everyone listening to their conversation.

'How many children did your father have?'

'Three,' Elizabeth replied. 'All lasses.'

'God be thanked,' the king replied with a smirk. 'If it had been three lads I'd have had no peace in my three kingdoms![1] They'd have all been just like their father and your husband.'

Elizabeth felt exasperated with these questions. They had nothing to do with her husband's exile. So she changed the subject, asking as politely as she could. 'Sir, I would like to request that you allow my husband to return to Scotland. He is very ill and his doctor says breathing his native air will help him.'

---

[1] The three kingdoms are England, Scotland and Ireland.

'Give him his native air? I'll give him the devil,' King James replied angrily.

Elizabeth was shocked. She had heard that the king was a profane man, but she thought he would not speak so in front of a Christian woman. And before she could stop her tongue, she replied, 'Is that how you speak to your courtiers?'

More gasps were heard around the room, and Elizabeth wondered if she had gone too far. Would the king put her in prison for her boldness, or maybe even worse?

The king studied Elizabeth in silence, and then smiled in an unsettling way.

'Very well, I will let your husband return to Scotland. On one condition. He must submit to bishops in the English church.'

Elizabeth was horrified. This was one of the reasons they had endured sixteen years of exile in France. The Bible said nothing about this kind of bishop in the church. And besides, the bishops just did as the king told them, so if John agreed to this, he would be choosing to follow the king instead of God.

'Never!' she replied, holding out her white apron. 'I'd rather see his head in my apron here than have him do that.'

'Then begone,' the king dismissed her. 'He can stay in London if he wants, but he may not return to Scotland.' And the king turned his back on Elizabeth and began to speak to a handsome young man.

Elizabeth almost said something more and then thought better of it. She had already said quite a bit to the king, more than most would ever dare. At least she and her family had won the right to stay in England and she was still free. The king could easily have put her in prison for her impudence.

When Elizabeth left the king's court, she went directly back to their lodgings. As she told her husband all that had been said and done at the court, a messenger arrived. The king's secretary sent a document giving John permission to preach in London. Elizabeth handed the stiff paper to her husband. 'Imagine him allowing you to preach and yet not to return to Scotland.'

John took the paper and read it for himself. 'I will take whatever opportunities God gives me. If this is where he wants me to preach, then I will. I must do God's work while he gives me strength.' He rose stiffly from his chair and reached for his Bible.

Elizabeth accompanied John to the church and she watched with a mixture of pride and worry as he climbed the steps to the pulpit. She offered a silent prayer, asking God to give him strength to preach.

And God did. John preached with more energy than she had seen in some time. The congregation was silent, listening carefully to every word. After a long time, John closed his sermon with prayer. And then he collapsed. It was as if he had used up all his strength on this one last sermon. Elizabeth was the first one out of her seat to be at his side. Gently several men lifted him up and carried John back to their lodgings. Elizabeth followed behind carrying his hat and cloak.

They laid him down in his bed and allowed Elizabeth to fuss over him, pulling up the covers and speaking softly to him. Louise and Nathaniel stood uncertainly near the door. Elizabeth knew John was dying, exhausted in his efforts to serve God even in poor health. She sat with him, listening to his muttered prayers as he drifted in and out of consciousness. She thought about what they had both risked to serve God over the years.

'Lord, your servant is a clay vessel and can hold no more,' John whispered.

Elizabeth caressed his forehead and prayed too, that God would grant her husband peace. An hour later he died quietly. Elizabeth knew he was now safe in God's hands, no longer suffering. The king may have kept John from returning to his home in Scotland, but God took him to the best home of all – to be in heaven with him.

Devotional Thought

I count everything as loss because of the surpassing worth of knowing Christ Jesus my Lord. For his sake I have suffered the loss of all things and count them as rubbish, in order that I may gain Christ and be found in him.

Philippians 3:8-9a

Elizabeth would have read these verses that the apostle Paul wrote and understood what Paul meant. Paul was telling the Philippian Christians that he was willing to give up everything he owned to serve Jesus. Paul was saying that everything else was like rubbish and not worth keeping if it interfered with serving God. Elizabeth knew what it was to give up everything she and John owned to serve God. She accepted being exiled from her home and country and having to move from place to place so her husband could preach the gospel in France. Nothing else mattered: not her house, her clothes, her belongings, or her friends. That took a great deal of courage. And Elizabeth needed courage to speak to the king, asking permission for her husband to return home to preach there. Like Paul, Elizabeth chose to serve God even though it meant leaving everything else behind.

Elizabeth was allowed to return home to Scotland after John died. She returned to Ayr, where John had been the minister for five years. She lived there for three years and then she died too. She lived long enough to know that her second son, Josiah, would carry on his father's work. He was ordained a minister and accepted a call to a church in Ireland just before Elizabeth died.

FRANCE

FACT FILE

This beautiful country is one of the most visited places in the world. France has an interesting history that goes back even before the time Julius Caesar conquered it for the Roman Empire.

France has the sixth largest economy in the world and has the third largest income in the world from tourism. The capital city is Paris. One of the most famous symbols of France, the Eiffel Tower stands at a staggering height of 984 feet, almost the height of a seventy storey building.

One of the largest art museums in the world, the Louvre, boasts of having some of the most prized artifacts. One of the most beautiful churches in France, the Cathedral of Notre Dame, is a classic example of a church built in the ancient Gothic style. It is located on a small island on the Seine River.

Great Britain and France in the 1600s

MARY SLESSOR

M ary was born in Aberdeen, Scotland on the 2nd of December, 1848. She moved to Dundee when she was eleven. Sadly her father was an alcoholic and lost his job, so Mary and her mother went out to work at the jute mill in Dundee. Mary worked half days at the mill and attended the mill school the other half. Mary's mother was a Christian and often read missionary stories to her children. When Mary became a

Christian, she promised God that she would become a missionary to Africa.

After Mary grew up, she applied to the Foreign Mission Board of the United Presbyterian Church. She trained for two years and then at the age of twenty-nine she sailed on a ship headed for the Calabar, what we call Nigeria today. It wasn't easy for a woman to be a missionary in that part of the world. There were many dangers, especially when she decided to go and live in the jungle instead of staying in the towns with the other missionaries. While in the jungle Mary was horrified to find that the Okoyong people had a number of violent customs. They thought twins were evil and they left them to die when they were born. Mary rescued a number of these abandoned children and raised them as her own. When she convinced the people that twins were not cursed, she became known as Ma Slessor, a title of honour among the people. The Okoyong people were very superstitious, believing in witchcraft and sorcery. Mary tried to stop these practices even though she was just one woman.

THE WARRING
TRIBES

(1890)

When Mary heard Janie, her adopted African daughter, cry, 'Run, Ma, Run!' she knew instantly that there was crisis. She leapt up from the mud stool by the fireplace in her bamboo mission house and grabbed her medicine bag.

Once outside, she met Mr. Ovens, a carpenter who had come to put doors and windows in her new house. He had heard the cry too. Together they plunged into the jungle surrounding the village of Chief Edem. As they ran they could hear cries of pain. A short way in they found a young man pinned beneath a tree trunk. Mary's heart still pounding from her sprint, now beat faster with fear.

'It's Chief Edem's son, Etim. Quick, get the tree off him.'

The three of them, man, woman and girl, struggled to shift the trunk and then Mary knelt beside him. Almost immediately she knew there was nothing in her medicine bag to help the young man. His eyes were open wide with fright and he couldn't move his arms or legs.

'We need a stretcher and some strong men to carry him,' Mary announced.

Janie left immediately to fetch more help while Mr. Ovens and Mary looked around for sturdy branches to turn into stretcher poles. Both of them were very worried.

'This will mean serious trouble,' Mr. Ovens whispered to Mary. 'If he dies, then someone will be blamed for witchcraft.'

Mary nodded. 'I don't think there is anything we can do for him. Poor Etim. He is to be married next week.'

Later with the help of some of the villagers, Etim was carried back to his father's house. For the next two weeks, Mary did her best to care for him. She gave him what medicine she had to ease his pain, but she could do nothing to take away the paralysis. In the end the young man died surrounded by the village folk.

In his grief, Chief Edem pushed Mary aside and called for the witchdoctor. He said, 'Sorcerers have killed my son and they must die!'

At those words everyone scattered into their houses or the jungle. They didn't want to be the ones accused. Only Mary and Mr. Ovens remained with the angry chief.

The witchdoctor arrived, wearing necklaces of small bones and paint on his face. He shook his rattles made from snake skins and small pebbles and began yelling and screaming. At last he stopped and announced, 'The village of Chief Akpo has done this!'

'No!' Mary said, but no one paid attention. Those who had been hiding now reappeared, and with loud voices echoed what the witchdoctor had said. They were relieved the witchdoctor hadn't named any of them. Then the warriors went to get their weapons to carry out the revenge.

'No!' Mary tried again. 'They had nothing to do with this. Please stop.' She ran after the warriors, but they ignored her and marched into the jungle.

The next day the warriors returned dragging a dozen miserable looking men, women and children from Chief Akpo's village. Mary stood at the door of her house surrounded by her five children, children she had rescued from death a few years before. What could she do to rescue those poor captives? Could she persuade Chief Edem that his son's death wasn't caused by these people?

As she watched them tie the captives to stakes in the centre of the village, an idea began to form in her mind. Since they were all upset over the young man's death, why not give him a good funeral? Maybe that would keep them away from the prisoners long enough to give Mary a chance to free them. So she went to a trunk full of clothing that the mission board had sent. From it she selected a suit and some silk to make a turban. When she arrived at the chief's house she explained that she wished to honour his son by dressing him well for his burial. Chief Edem agreed and allowed Mary to put on the clothing. Then the chief called all the villagers together and supplied them with food and drink. Unfortunately, the drink was liquor and very quickly the funeral became a loud, ugly party.

Mary left the drinking and dancing crowd and met Mr. Ovens, who was standing guard over the prisoners. 'You must stay here with them. The villagers are very drunk now and may try to kill the captives immediately.'

Mr. Ovens agreed. 'But where are you going?' he asked Mary.

'To look for the poisoned beans,' Mary replied with determination. 'I overheard the chief's brother say they are going to give them to the captives tomorrow. They say if the captives are innocent, they won't die from the poison, but, of course, that's not true. I've got to save these people somehow.'

As the loud party continued Mary crept into the house of the witchdoctor, looking for the beans. She found them sitting on a pounding stone, ready to be pounded into powder and put into cups of water that each prisoner would have to drink. She quickly gathered them up and was ready to return to her own house when she heard her name being called out.

Rushing back to the centre of the village she found Mr. Ovens trying to hold off several of the drunken warriors from killing the prisoners with their knives.

'Stop!' Mary shouted in the loudest voice she could. 'Stop it now!' And she pushed her way through the warriors and stood between them and the prisoners. Arms folded across her chest, Mary glared at the men, all the while praying that God would protect her.

Stunned, everyone stood still. Then Chief Edem arrived. 'You must let my men do their work. My son's death must be avenged,' he argued.

Mary shook her head vigorously. 'These people are innocent. To kill them is murder and against God's law. And I will sit here with them until you let them all go.' Then Mary went and sat down among the prisoners. How out of place Mary looked, a small white woman with red hair among the tall dark prisoners.

The warriors looked at their chief and lowered their weapons. They respected Ma Slessor because of everything she had done to help their people. She had taught their children in school, doctored them when they were ill, showed them how to trade with their neighbours, and taught them about God. They didn't want to harm her. And they couldn't kill the prisoners without accidentally killing her.

Chief Edem was angry with Mary, but also fearful of upsetting the other missionaries who came to his village on occasion. He also knew Mary had a powerful friend, King Eyo Honesty VII, who lived down the river. The king had become a Christian and helped the missionaries. So the chief called his warriors off, but not without a stern warning to Mary.

'I will have my revenge, and I might just get it by burning down your house.'

Mary gasped, knowing the chief was trying to get her to leave the prisoners to save her house and her children. Quickly she prayed and then called out to the chief.

'Let me have three of the prisoners. Let them stay in my house and Mr. Ovens will make sure they don't run away.'

Before the chief could speak, his sister Ma Eme stepped forward to plead with her brother. Ma Eme had become Mary's closest friend in the village. 'Please, brother, do as Ma Slessor asks. You know she is an honourable woman. And you will still have the other prisoners.'

Reluctantly he agreed, and before he could change his mind Mary untied the ropes holding a young mother and her two children. 'Go quickly,' she urged them. 'Mr. Ovens will take you to safety.' Then Mary settled back down on the ground in the middle of the prisoners. She wasn't moving, for she knew if she did, the prisoners would be killed.

Chief Edem stomped away to his house while the villagers all drifted back to their homes too. Only a few warriors remained as guards while the cool night fell.

Mary had spent many nights like this over the years out in the open, sleeping on the hard ground. Overhead the dark sky was filled with stars and all around the noises of the jungle night filled the air. She couldn't sleep, so she used the time to pray. She asked God for protection for her and her family and all these prisoners. She knew very well the chief could order her death and in the end his warriors would obey him. Only God could stop them. Then she asked for wisdom to know what to do next. Somehow she had to convince Chief Edem and his village that believing in witchcraft was wrong.

The next day Chief Edem demanded that Mr. Ovens make a coffin for his son. It was time for the burial. Mr. Ovens knew this wasn't a good thing. If the people believed someone had died from witchcraft then they could only be buried after the accused person had been killed. The chief must be planning to kill the other prisoners. So Mr. Ovens decided to bargain.

'I'll make the coffin if you free some more prisoners. I'll see they are kept in Ma Slessor's house.'

The chief was torn. He wanted to bury his son, and he wanted to kill the prisoners. 'You may have three more,' he finally replied.

When Mary heard the news she untied six more and sent them off with Mr. Ovens before anyone noticed how many. Once more she sat down with the three remaining prisoners. She felt hungry and tired and her back ached from the hard ground. *Thank you, Lord*, she prayed quietly. *Please help us to save the rest.*

Mr. Ovens took his time building the coffin. Many of the men of the village gathered round to watch, casting glances over at Mary and the prisoners. Mary was trying to comfort the two frightened young men and one woman.

When the coffin was finished, the chief's son was laid gently in it. Mary watched from a distance, her heart pounding. Now was the time for the prisoners to die. She stood up stiffly, very weary from her days and nights of 'guarding' the prisoners. Gathering all her strength, she placed herself in front of them and stood firm.

'You must not kill them,' she said, looking Chief Edem in the eye. He glared back at her and the entire village waited in silence.

Just at that the moment noises were heard on the far side of the village that led down to the river. As everyone turned to look, two missionaries carrying suitcases entered the village. Behind them trailed their Okoyong guides.

'We made it safely up the river,' one of the young men called out cheerfully. 'Even if there were more crocodiles than I had ever seen before.'

The villagers hesitated and then went to greet the new arrivals. Chief Edem, seeing his people were distracted, broke off his stare with Mary and turned to meet the missionaries as they came to stand by him.

'My friends in Duke Town send their greetings to you and your village,' the young man said. 'We received a message some time ago saying that your people would like to see our magic lantern show. I've brought it with me,' he said tapping

his suitcase. 'Once it gets dark this evening, I can show you the pictures.'

Mary sighed with relief. This was just the distraction the village needed. The missionaries could show their slides of various places around the world and keep the villagers calm and interested. Maybe then Chief Edem would see reason and let the last of the prisoners go.

That evening the entire village gathered round for the slide show, expressing wonder at the 'magic' pictures. Meanwhile Mary sat with the prisoners praying desperately that God would change the heart of the chief.

God answered Mary's prayer. The next morning Chief Edem stood before Mary and the entire village. 'I want to bury my son. I will let the prisoners go. Instead I will kill a cow. That way blood will be shed for my son and he can be buried. I do this for you Ma Slessor. It's more than I have ever done for anyone else.'

With great relief Mary fell down on her knees and thanked God right in front of the whole village. As she stood up she bowed to the chief. 'Thank you,' she said. And then taking the opportunity that God had made for her, she told the whole village again about how God had sacrificed his own son to pay the penalty for their sin. Some believed that day and became Christians.

Devotional Thought:

Have I not commanded you? Be strong and courageous. Do not be frightened, and do not be dismayed, for the LORD *your God is with you wherever you go.*

Joshua 1:9

God said these words to Joshua as he was preparing to lead the people of Israel into battle to claim the promised land. That was a job that required courage and knowing that God was with him. Mary Slessor would have read these words in her Bible and understood how Joshua must have felt. She had to have courage in a very dangerous situation as she faced Chief Edem and his warriors. She stood with the prisoners not knowing if the chief would order her death as well. But she knew, as Joshua did, that God always keeps his promises. God had promised to be with Joshua, and with all those who love and serve him. He was with Mary as she stood up for what was right, even if it meant she might die. And God has promised to be with us wherever we go, if we are following his commands.

Mary spent the rest of her life in the Calabar, rescuing children, caring for the people and teaching the gospel. She gained so much respect that the British government even appointed her a magistrate for the area to help settle disputes among the people. Mary returned to Scotland for several visits, bringing some of her children with her each time. She visited many churches, telling them of the needs in Africa and encouraging them to support missionaries. After her last visit home in 1910 she moved even deeper into the jungle where no missionaries had gone before, and she spent her last fifteen years telling as many people as she could about God's love and their need for salvation.

NIGERIA

FACT FILE

Nigeria is located in the region of Western Africa, bordered by the Gulf of Guinea, Benin, Niger and Cameroon. The country consists of lowlands near the coast, rising to plateaus and mountains towards the interior. The major rivers are the Niger and Benue. The Niger enters the country from the northwest and flows southward through tropical rain forests and swamps to its delta on the coast.

Nigerian's official language is English, but the people also speak several native languages. Nigeria is the most populous country in Africa with 250 ethnic or tribal groups. Forty percent of the people call themselves Christian, while fifty percent are Muslim and ten percent practice native religions.

Nigeria has rich deposits of oil and natural gas, iron ore and coal. The country is subject to periodic droughts and flooding.

Nigeria in the 1800s

MILDRED CABLE

ildred lived from 1878 to 1952. She was born in Guildford, England, and became a Christian as a young teen. When she heard a missionary speak of God's love for the lost, she promised God to go wherever he wanted her to go. Mildred applied to the China Inland Mission when she was twenty-one, but before going to China she studied to be a chemist, and also studied nursing. When she arrived in China she met Eva French, another missionary who had already travelled from village to village in northern China sharing the gospel. The two became close friends. Later Eva's sister, Francesca, joined them and together they become known as The Trio. The three women began missionary journeys outside the Great Wall of China where few missionaries had gone. With only donkey-pulled carts full of Bibles and Christian books, they travelled thousands of miles across the Gobi Desert, 'gossiping the gospel' to the Chinese, Mongolian and Turkistani women they met. They offered friendship and medical help wherever they went, taking every opportunity to present the love of God to the women and children. They faced physical hardship and danger in their wilderness wanderings, and none was more dangerous than their last journey. They became trapped in Tunhwang, also known as the City of Sands, when the rebel warlord General Ma captured the city during a rampage across the Gobi Desert.

CAPTURED!

NOVEMBER 1931

The mayor of the City of Sands announced, 'There is terrible news,' as he stood just inside the small house that the missionaries had rented.

Mildred exchanged a worried glance with Eva, while Francesca stopped the washing-up to listen. All three women were in their fifties and had been missionaries in China and the Gobi Desert for over thirty years. This was the first time they had become directly involved in a war.

The mayor continued, 'The General has come back to Ansi.'

Mildred could have smiled at that if she hadn't been so worried. Ansi, also known as the City of Peace, was an odd place for the cruel warlord to make his headquarters.

'And he's wounded.' The mayor nervously pulled out a letter from his quilted jacket. 'He demands that two of you go with his soldiers to be his doctors.'

Mildred's eyes opened wide with fear. They had managed to stay safely in their little house even during the last few months that the city had been under siege. The rebel soldiers had taken most of the food that had been grown in the beautiful oasis surrounding the city, and anything else they took a fancy to. And almost daily someone was taken off as a prisoner, usually men and boys to be pressed into the rebel army. Mildred knew if the soldiers separated them, the women might never see each other again.

'No, you can't separate us,' Eva announced.

'I can't disobey the General,' the mayor replied. 'He'll burn the city.'

'Don't worry.' Mildred explained, patting the anxious man on the arm. 'We'll all go. We'll take our own cart and supplies, but you will have to give us some donkeys, as the General's men have already taken ours some days ago,' she finished with annoyance. She looked over at Francesca and Eva, who both nodded. Even nine-year-old Topsy, Mildred's adopted daughter, came over and slipped her hand into Mildred's.

Relieved, the mayor agreed to find them the animals and some medical supplies. Mildred knew he wouldn't find much, but even some bandages would be helpful. After she showed the mayor out, she pushed up her wire-rimmed glasses on her nose and began to think about what they could manage to pack up quickly before the soldiers hustled them away.

In the midst of the hasty preparations, Topsy pulled on Mildred's arm. Mildred saw the anxious look on her daughter's face and dropped the last of the clothing into the box.

'Come over here,' Mildred said, making sure Topsy could see her face. Mildred spoke slowly and clearly so Topsy could read her lips because the girl was both deaf and mute. Mildred sat down on a bench and explained that they had to go to Ansi to help the wounded General. It would take four days to get there and she must be patient and obedient for her own safety. Topsy nodded with understanding, her long dark braids swinging along her back, and then she moved closer for a reassuring hug from Mildred.

Early the next morning several soldiers arrived to lead the women, their cart and carter out of the city. As they passed through the city gate, Mildred saw a large group of prisoners, men and boys, whom the soldiers had rounded up. They were in chains and some had been beaten.

47

'Look at those poor boys,' Francesca whispered as she pointed to two older boys who were weeping. A soldier rode by them on horseback and swung a long stick at them, clipping one on the side of the head. A man, who was probably a relative, started to shout and had to be held back by other prisoners from trying to pull the soldier off his horse. More soldiers rode over and more blows rained down on the prisoners.

Topsy buried her head in Mildred's long Chinese tunic of blue cotton. 'There, there,' Mildred said, knowing that Topsy couldn't hear her, but needing to reassure herself too.

The journey was very difficult. The poor sad donkeys that the mayor had found for them (more likely stolen, Eva had muttered) could barely manage to pull the cart, never mind any passengers. So the women and Topsy trudged along behind, all the while trying to keep clear of the stick swinging soldiers on horseback. The November nights were cold in the desert, and when they made camp the women huddled around a small fire drinking tea and eating their ration of bread. Wrapped up in quilts, they slept on the ground by their cart.

As the bedraggled parade of prisoners and missionaries arrived at the walled City of Peace, the soldiers shouted for the gates to be opened. A young soldier of about fifteen stepped out holding a gun and began to question them.

'You there,' he called out to the missionary women. 'Who are you? Show me your passports,' he demanded.

They each took out their British passports and handed them to the sneering young man. 'Wait here,' he ordered, and disappeared back inside the city. The women stood shivering in the cold wind and waited, while all around them the prisoners were being taken away.

Eventually the young man returned with a group of equally rough-looking men who waved their guns and shouted at them to follow. Mildred called to the carter to follow them into the city. As the parade of soldiers, missionaries and their cart wound through the street, Mildred saw that this was no longer a place of peace. Thin, hungry looking children peered out of doorways, while here and there a woman or an old man lay slumped against a wall, some reeking of opium. Mildred's heart ached for them. With no food, the people were turning to the drug to ease their pain.

The group came to stop in front of a school. The young man shouted at them to go inside and Mildred ventured in first, with Topsy clinging to her side. They were shown into a classroom and told they could sleep here.

'Not much of a place,' Eva remarked acidly in English as she followed Mildred.

'Never mind,' her sister, Francesca, said. 'We'll make it homely. At least it's out of the wind.'

'You may have rations from the General's stores. Send that man to get them,' the young soldier barked as the carter entered the room. 'The General will see you tomorrow morning. Be ready.'

Mildred sent the carter off to get the rations, while the women and Topsy did what they could with the bedding and clothing they brought to make the room comfortable. When the carter returned, he brought a bag of millet and news that he'd found a stable for the donkeys, but no food for them. Mildred just shook her head.

'There's nothing we can do about that. Come in, and eat with us. We'll make a soup with this millet and some tea. We've made up a place for you to sleep over there in the corner.'

The next morning the women rose stiffly from their beds on the floor, rolled up their blankets and turned on their little camp stove to make tea. But there was no time to drink it. The young soldier was back banging on the door. Mildred put on her coat and picked up her bag of medical supplies. Eva and Francesca also came, leaving Topsy in the care of the carter.

The soldier led them to the best house in the city. They were ushered into a room full of rough-looking soldiers, all wearing turbans and carrying weapons. Mildred chose to ignore the men, focusing instead on the young man seated on a dais at the end of the room. The dais was covered in rich rugs and the walls around it were hung with British guns. In the centre sat the General, a tall graceful man of about twenty. A cheerful fire blazed in a brazier nearby.

'He disobeyed me. I want him shot,' the General said to one of the soldiers, as calmly as if he were discussing the weather. The soldier departed to carry out the instructions.

The General, seeing Mildred and her companions, motioned them forward with a lazy hand. 'So you are to be my doctors,' he announced.

Then Mildred noticed his bandaged legs. The bandages were dirty and crusted with blood. 'These need to be changed,' she said.

'Of course,' the General agreed. 'But you must not hurt me. I don't want any more pain.'

Mildred took a deep breath. 'I'll try to be as gentle as possible,' she said as she knelt down on the step of the dais and opened her bag. She took out a small pair of scissors and began to carefully cut away the old bandages. As she worked, she realized that the General was carrying on with his business as usual,

giving orders and discussing strategy. When she poured the disinfectant on the unhealed gunshot wounds, the General gasped and tried to slap her. Mildred pulled back in time and apologised.

'That was necessary,' she explained. 'We must be sure that there is no infection. I won't need to do that again today.' Then she carefully wrapped each leg in clean bandages. 'I will need to come tomorrow to change the bandages again,' she said, standing up and putting her supplies away.

'Yes, yes,' the General replied impatiently. 'Now go away.'

And so it went for many days; the three women arrived at the General's house, Mildred changed the bandages, and then they returned to their schoolroom lodging. There was less food each day and the uncertainty of the General's temper and his soldiers made life very uneasy. Mildred, Eva and Francesca spent their time getting to know the people living around them, offering them friendship and medical care. Even some of the rebel soldiers began to come to them for help. The women also spent time reading their Bibles and praying. They were especially praying that God would show them how to escape. For once the General's wounds had healed he would have no further use for them. Then what would become of them?

One day the General's chief of staff paid them a surprise visit. The women offered him tea and to their delight discovered he could speak French. This meant they could have a private discussion that the other soldiers couldn't understand. Mildred felt the prompting of the Holy Spirit telling her to ask the man for a permit to travel. So as the women chatted to him, Mildred suddenly said, 'Would it be possible for my friends and me to leave the city? The General is almost well and no longer needs my care.'

The chief of staff was thoughtful. 'Leave it with me. I'll see what can be done.'

After he left, Mildred, Eva and Francesca spent a long time praying that God would give the man courage and opportunity to get the permit.

A few days later the chief of staff returned. He bowed respectfully to the three women and then pulled out a document from his jacket pocket with a smile. 'This allows you to leave this city, but you must not leave the oasis area. If you do then you could be shot on sight.'

Mildred was so relieved she could have hugged the man, but that would not be proper. Instead, she thanked him as best she could with words. They began to pack up their belongings immediately in case anyone should arrive to take back the permit.

'The donkeys that brought us here can no longer pull a cart,' the carter informed them sadly. 'They have not been fed properly at all. But,' he added, 'I've found the very donkeys the soldiers stole from us when we were in Tunhwang, the City of Sands, and they have been very well fed. They're strong and able to pull our cart. Shall I take them instead?' he asked hopefully.

'I don't see why not,' Eva replied, looking at Mildred. 'After all, they are our donkeys.'

Mildred laughed. 'Yes,' she said. 'And it was kind of the General's men to take care of them for us.'

The carter grinned and went off to secure the animals to their cart.

But just as the group was ready to leave the city, a message arrived to say that the General wanted to see them. The women looked at each other with anxious faces. Did this mean their permit had been cancelled?

'We'd better go,' Francesca said. 'Otherwise the guards won't even let us out of the gate.'

'Yes, but we mustn't say anything about the permit,' Eva replied. 'You know how easily he flies into a temper. We don't want to provoke him in any way.'

Mildred said nothing, but before they headed to the General's house, she picked up a New

Testament and a small booklet containing the Ten Commandments.

The Trio were shown into the General's audience room immediately. The young man was standing, his legs now fully healed, speaking with one of his aides. He beckoned them forward and the crowd of soldiers broke apart to allow them through. Mildred stepped to the front.

'Your wounds are better now?' she inquired.

'Yes,' the General replied with a smile that wasn't precisely friendly. 'You have done well. And I understand you have healed some of my soldiers from their wounds too.'

'No,' Mildred replied. 'God does the healing. I simply do the nursing.' Then taking a deep breath, she continued. 'You should take note of what God has done for you. More than your legs need to be healed. You need to take care of your soul. Here is a copy of God's Word, along with a copy of His Law. You should read these and then repent of your sin. You need to follow the true and living God.'

The General stood very still, while his soldiers stirred uneasily. No one had ever had the courage to say such things before. Mildred might just have lost her opportunity to leave the city safely, and maybe even her life. She stood as bravely as she could waiting for the General's reaction.

The General said nothing. Instead he saluted the women and waved them out of his presence. Mildred set the New Testament and the Ten Commandment booklet down on a table and followed Eva and Francesca out of the room.

Once out on the street Mildred found she was shaking, while the other two hugged her fiercely. Then they were aware that the chief of staff had followed them out.

'Go,' he urged them. 'Get out now, in case he changes his mind.'

They did as he said and ran to the waiting cart. Climbing up and sitting with Topsy and the carter on top of their belongings, Mildred told the carter to move the donkeys quickly. They almost forgot to breathe until they were safely past the gate and once more on the open road.

'Go along a piece,' Mildred said to the carter as they bounced along, 'until we are out of sight. Then turn off and head out into the desert.'

'But we were told to stay on the main road and go to the oasis,' he said.

'We won't,' she replied. 'There are many villages yet to visit. Many people who still need to hear the gospel. That's where we will go.'

Devotional Thought:

Blessed be the LORD, *the God of Israel, who alone does wondrous things. Blessed be his glorious name forever; may the whole earth be filled with his glory!*
Amen and Amen!
Psalm 72:18–19

Mildred and her friends, Eva and Francesca, would have read these verses in Psalm 72 and agreed with them with all their hearts. God did a wondrous thing in delivering them safely from the rebel, General Ma. And they were sure to bless or praise God for his goodness and care, even as they continued to visit the villages in the desert while evading the rebels. They hoped to see many people come to faith.

It's important to recognize all the wonderful things God does for us; not just the big spectacular things, but all the day to day things too. He gives us our health. He gives us families to care for us. He gives us many material blessings that we just think we ought to have. All good things come from God and that is wonderful because we don't really deserve any of it. Even though we are like mere ants in God's sight, he has shown us great love, especially by sending his Son to us. How much we should be praising God and wanting to see others praising him too.

Mildred, her friends, and daughter travelled a long way through the desert until they finally came to the border of Russia. Once there they took a train to Moscow and then across Europe and home to England. They had many stories to tell and Mildred and Francesca decided to write books to tell them. They shared their exciting adventures in the desert and praised God for his many wondrous works.

GOBI DESERT

FACT FILE

The Gobi Desert is the second largest desert in Asia (after the Arabian Desert) and is the fourth largest desert in the world. It covers parts of both northern China and southern Mongolia and is about 500,000 square miles in size. The Gobi has temperatures ranging from minus 40 degrees in winter to 113 degrees in the summer.

The Gobi is a very dry and windy desert. Some regions of the desert average two to eight inches of rain a year, however, other regions may go years without rainfall. Sand storms present a great danger in the Gobi; winds can reach 85 miles per hour.

It is estimated that the Gobi holds the world's richest and most diverse deposits of dinosaur and early mammal remains.

The Great Gobi National Park contains the last remaining wild Bacterian (two-humped) camels. Other animals inhabiting the Gobi are wild asses, Saiga antelopes, wild horses, and the only desert dwelling bear.

Map of China in the 1900s

GLADYS AYLWARD

Gladys was born in London, England in 1902 into a working class family. Because her family had little money to spend on Gladys' schooling, she had to go out to work as a parlour maid when she was fourteen. When Gladys turned eighteen she attended a revival meeting and was converted. From that time onward, she felt a call to be a missionary. She decided to continue in her job and save her earnings so she could go to the mission field. When she was twenty-six, she applied to a mission board but they said 'No' because she had so little schooling. Several years later, in 1932, Gladys decided to go anyway. She began a long train journey across Europe and Asia with one suitcase and £2 9p in her pocket. God kept her safe through many difficulties and she ended up in the town of Yangcheng in China, anxious to serve God and tell others about him.

For eight years she shared the good news of Jesus Christ with the Chinese people by managing an inn and travelling to remote mountain villages. Many people had come to faith and now most of the villages in the area had a small Christian community. God had blessed Gladys' work. But now there was a war.

THE LONG PARADE OVER THE MOUNTAINS

1940

Gladys ran for cover as the bullets showered down around her. She dodged back and forth as she hurried up the hillside, crouching behind bushes and rocks. She pulled off her padded jacket, rolled it into a ball and pitched it one way while she ran the other. The bullets tore into the discarded jacket as Gladys dropped behind a bush a few metres away. Breathing heavily, she closed her eyes for a moment. *Please God, keep me safe*, she prayed. Then Gladys crawled, crept, ran and climbed until eventually she sank to the ground behind some large rocks. The Japanese soldiers finally gave up and returned to the city below.

Gladys fell asleep behind the rocks and slept undisturbed for several hours in her hiding place.

When she awoke she shivered, wishing she still had her warm padded coat. The sun had gone down, leaving dark shadows and a cool breeze. But she felt refreshed, so she started to climb the rest of the way up the mountain. She knew of a small village nestled among the peaks that would shelter her for the night. Then she would have to walk for another day to reach her children, waiting for her at the Inn of the Eight Happinesses.

The Japanese had invaded China from the north, marching southward through the mountains. Four times the town of Yangcheng had been captured by the enemy, and four times the Chinese National Army drove them back. In the midst of all that fighting, Gladys and other missionaries cared for the wounded and orphans and shared God's Word. Enemy soldiers allowed them to do this, thinking the 'foreign devils' were no threat to them. After all, the missionaries weren't soldiers and didn't carry weapons. Then the Japanese found out that Gladys was also a spy! When she visited the village churches, she noted the location of the Japanese troops and reported the information to the Chinese army. The Japanese were angry! They offered £100 to whoever would capture her. So now Gladys was on the run, trying to avoid the Japanese soldiers as she continued to visit the villages and towns. They had almost caught her that time. Maybe now it was time to move to a safer place, especially because of the children.

'Ai-weh-deh!' fifteen-year-old Ninepence shouted as Gladys walked through the inn door two days later. She rushed into Gladys' open arms and squeezed her tight. Ninepence was Gladys' first adopted child. So many people had been killed in the war that over a hundred children had come to Gladys' inn to live. They slept in the various buildings and courtyard of the Inn of the Eight Happinesses.

'Ai-weh-deh!' Gladys' Chinese name was repeated over and over as the Chinese children crowded around her. The older ones wanted hugs just like the little ones. They all spoke at once until the noise was too much even for Gladys, who was overjoyed to see her children safe.

'Enough,' she called out, laughing as a three-year-old pushed his way through the legs of the older ones. He caught Gladys around the legs and held on tight. Gladys bent down and picked up the pudgy boy. With her free arm she signalled the chattering crowd to be quiet.

'Yes, God has kept me safe. And you too. We have much to thank him for, even in the middle of war.' She began to move about the group, patting heads and squeezing arms, murmuring encouraging words to as many as she could.

As she reached the doorway into the kitchen area, she set the boy down and bowed to Yang, her cook and mission helper. 'Thank you for all you have done while I've been away, my friend. Have I arrived in time for dinner?' she asked with a smile.

Yang shook his head, his long pigtail swinging across his back. Wearing his usual worried expression he replied, 'All we have is some millet. I've cooked it up into a thin porridge that I hope will feed everyone. Food is so scarce, Ai-weh-deh. I don't know what we'll do.'

'You won't need to worry after tonight,' Gladys replied. 'I'm taking the children away from here. It's no longer safe for them while the Japanese are looking for me. And you're right. There isn't enough food. It's either been destroyed by the bombs or taken by the soldiers.' Then Gladys turned once more to the children. Not all could fit inside the main hall of the inn, so they were hanging off the staircase or crowding in around the open doors and windows. 'Let's all go out into the courtyard,' she motioned with her hands. 'And allow Yang to get on with our meal. I have something to tell you.'

The children all surged toward the doors, the older ones making way for the little ones. They assembled in the courtyard and sat down.

'This is what we are going to do. First we must worship God. He has kept us safe, even with bombs and guns all around us. Then we will eat and have a long sleep. Tomorrow morning we are going on a long walk, all the way to Sian. We'll be safe there.'

They sang a hymn and Gladys prayed. Then she told them the familiar story of Jesus feeding the five thousand, reminding them that God cared for each one of them. Afterwards they ate their small meal and the children settled down for the night, wrapped in their blankets in every nook and cranny of the inn. Then Gladys met Yang in the kitchen to discuss her plans.

'You can't do this, Ai-weh-deh,' Yang said mournfully. 'You have no money, no food. How will you care for the children on the journey? And how will you get there with the enemy looking for you on every road?'

'God will provide,' Gladys answered with certainty. 'I will speak to the Mandarin at first light and ask if he can spare any supplies for us. And we won't take any of the roads. We'll go through the mountains, along paths that I know but the Japanese do not. Don't forget, I've travelled through those mountains for eight years now. I'm sure we will find a safe way.'

Yang shook his head doubtfully. 'I hope you're right,' he said.

The next morning at dawn the children laughed and talked excitedly in the courtyard of the inn. They could hardly wait to start their long walk. Each had a blanket rolled up with a bowl and chopsticks inside. Ninepence and Sualan, along with the other older girls and boys, went about helping the youngest ones roll their blankets more securely.

Gladys entered the courtyard from the street with two Chinese soldiers and blew her whistle. The children stopped at once and waited to hear what Ai-weh-deh would say.

'Children, you must line up now, like a parade. It's time to leave. These soldiers will be coming with us as far as the first village. Our Mandarin has kindly lent them to us and also given us some food for our journey. Now come along, we have a long way to go.'

The children did as they were told, although Ninepence and Sualan had to scoop up a couple of the three-year-olds and carry them. People lined the streets to watch as the children cheerfully waved goodbye and followed Gladys out of the city gates toward the mountains.

At first it all seemed like a great adventure. The children enjoyed the warm sunny day, and the freedom to run and climb and explore as they moved up into the mountains. When they came to a flat plateau with a running stream, they cooked up the millet in the big iron pot that the soldiers carried for them. After their picnic, they washed their bowls in the stream and started on their journey again.

As Gladys led them up a track used by mules, little San pulled on her grey cotton tunic. 'Ai-weh-deh, I'm tired,' the four-year-old girl announced. 'Will you carry me?'

Gladys smiled and reached down. 'Of course, little one.' Together they led the parade of children. Soon other young children begged the older ones to carry them too.

By the end of the day, everyone was tired and glad to stumble into a village nestled in the mountains. The villagers had only a little food themselves, so they were relieved that Gladys came with her own. That night Gladys led the entire village in evening devotions before everyone settled down for the night.

Awake at first light, the parade of children formed up again. But this time they said goodbye to the Mandarin's soldiers. Instead, two men from the village offered to accompany the children to their next stop. And so it went; long days of walking, running and climbing through the mountain passes, moving from village to village. Not everyone was happy to see them. Many villages had no food to share, or places for them to sleep. So Gladys and her children slept out in courtyards, small meadows or caves, wherever there was room enough for them all to lie down. The nights were cold and sometimes one blanket wasn't enough, so the children began to sleep in close huddles, cuddling into each other to keep warm. Once a Buddhist priest saw them and offered them his temple to sleep in. Gladys gratefully accepted the offer. How much better the children would be able to walk the next day if they had a warm place to sleep.

By the sixth day the sense of adventure was wearing off. Their food supplies were running low and many of their cloth shoes had started to come apart on the rugged pathways.

'Ai-weh-deh, my feet hurt,' eight-year-old Lufu cried, the soles of his shoes flapping each time he took a step.

'I'm hungry,' little San whined.

'Will the long walk be over soon?' Liang asked. 'I'm tired of walking.'

'Let's sing,' Gladys called out, hoping to distract the children from their difficulties. She began to sing 'Count your blessings, name them one by one,' and the children joined in. Gladys felt tears begin to form in her eyes as the children sang the last stanza.

> *So, amid the conflict whether great or small,*
> *Do not be disheartened, God is over all;*
> *Count your many blessings, angels will attend,*
> *Help and comfort give you to your journey's end.*

Please give us your help and comfort, Lord, she prayed.

That night as the younger children settled down to sleep, Gladys called the older children to her. Twenty girls and seven boys ranging in age from eleven to sixteen gathered round her.

Gladys looked round the circle of tired faces, knowing they still had a long way to go. 'The pathways are becoming more difficult, especially for the little ones. I will need you girls to help them. I know you have been trying your best, so all you need to do is keep on doing it. Boys', she said, turning to them, 'I have a special job for you. Liang and Teh, I want you to be our advanced scouts. You go ahead of the group and look for the best pathways for the little ones. Also I need you to keep a lookout for soldiers. Don't forget we are at war. The rest of you boys will be at the head of our group, ready to defend us, so find some large sticks to carry.'

The children all nodded seriously.

'Ai-weh-deh,' Less spoke up. 'We found some white paint in the last village that no one wanted. Could Liang and Teh use that to leave signs for us, so we know the right path to take?'

The boys nodded vigorously. 'We could paint the rocks!'

'Wonderful idea,' Gladys agreed. 'Now off to bed with you.'

The next day the older boys took the lead while Liang and Teh ran on ahead. As the group walked along, Gladys explained what the white painted rocks meant, and it became a game to follow them. Then someone noticed a word on one rock and another next to it.

Gladys called out the words, 'Bless the Lord.'

One of the children near the back of the line replied, 'O my soul.'

Then another called out, 'And all that is within me.'

'Praise his Holy name,' several voices finished.

And so the game of bible verses began, some left by the advance scouts on the rocks and some Gladys began on her own. The day passed quickly.

The next day began as all the others had, with a little bit of food for breakfast and a long weary climb through the mountains. Again the scouts left painted clues, but then in mid-afternoon Liang and Teh suddenly appeared, running up to Gladys.

'Ai-weh-deh,' Liang began, panting from his long run. 'Soldiers!'

Gladys's heart started to pound. Were there really Japanese soldiers so far up here in the mountains? Before she could call the children to her with her whistle, two soldiers appeared around a bend in the path. For several seconds Gladys forgot to breathe and then suddenly she relaxed. The men wore Chinese army uniforms, not Japanese.

The captain looked at the crowd of children in amazement. Then seeing that Gladys was the only adult, he made his way over to her. 'What are you doing here?' he asked.

'I'm taking these children to the orphanage in Sian where they will be safe from the fighting,' Gladys replied.

'How many?' he asked.

'Only a hundred,' Gladys said with a smile.

The captain's eyes widened with surprise. 'My men are camped in the clearing not far from here. You should join us for the night.'

'Do you have any food?' Liang asked quietly.

The captain nodded. 'We'll share with you.'

'Bless you,' Gladys said, suddenly very tired.

What a wonderful night they all had. The soldiers, far from home and their own families, were glad to see the children. They shared their food, told them stories, and tucked them up in their blankets to sleep for the night. In the morning, Gladys thanked the captain for his generosity and kindness and then led the children on their walk again.

For twelve days the children walked until at last they came to the Yellow River. What a sight it was, a wide swiftly flowing river that gleamed like a golden ribbon in the sunlight. The children cheered, thinking that at last they had come to the end. Gladys said nothing, but urged them down the mountain side, hoping the town of Yuan Chu by the river had some food to share with her hungry, tired children.

As they walked into the town, there was silence.

'Where is everyone?' Sualan whispered.

Shifting a sleeping toddler on her hip, Gladys wrapped her free arm around the teenager. 'Gone,' she replied. 'They must have fled from the Japanese.' How was she going to feed all these children? And how would they cross that mighty river? All the boats were gone. Gladys had a sudden urge to sit down and cry. Had they come all this way to be left to wait for the Japanese army to capture them?

The children searched the empty houses and found small items of food that had been left behind. They gathered them all up, put them in the iron pot to cook with some well water and had a very thin soup for supper. Gladys had never felt so dejected and alone, even surrounded by so many children. She was even too discouraged to pray. So she sat on a rock by the river, staring out into the distance.

'Ai-weh-deh,' Sualan's voice sounded near her. 'We have finished bathing the little children and they're all in their blankets now. Will we cross the river tomorrow?'

Gladys shook her head. 'There are no boats.'

Sualan sat down. 'But Ai-weh-deh, why don't we ask God to part the water?' Gladys looked at the girl with amazement. Sualan continued. 'You've told us the story of Moses and the Red Sea many, many times. Don't you believe it? Didn't God really help the Israelites? Why can't we ask him to help us?'

Gladys started to cry. Through her tears she reached out and hugged the concerned teenager. 'You have more faith than I do, my daughter. Of course we should ask God. Call all the older children here and we'll pray right now.'

A few minutes later they were kneeling in a group by the shore of the river, asking God to provide a way across. They ended by singing songs of praise to God.

Suddenly they heard a noise nearby. A Chinese soldier had heard their singing and was walking towards them. Gladys urged the children to stand behind her as the man stopped in front of her.

'What are you doing here?' he demanded. 'Everyone has run away. The Japanese will be here very soon. Why are you still here?'

'We came across the mountains,' Gladys explained. 'Now we need to cross the river.'

The soldier looked at all the children. 'Are all these yours? They walked across the mountains?' He shook his head in disbelief 'You foolish woman. I should leave you here for the Japanese to find.' Then his face softened. 'I will call the boats, but you must be quick. I don't want any boats left here for the enemy to use when they arrive.'

Gladys smiled and the children began to cheer. God had answered their prayer. The soldier blew a special code on his whistle and boats arrived a short time later. Gladys woke the younger children up. It took several trips across the river to land everyone safe on the other side.

The people in the village had plenty to share, taking children into their homes and letting them eat their fill of food. Happy and full to bursting, the children slept well that night. Before she went to sleep Gladys prayed. *Thank you, Lord for taking care of us on our journey. Just like you led the Israelites through the Red sea and the wilderness, please continue to be with us until we reach our destination.*

Devotional Thought:

Do not be anxious about anything, but in everything by prayer and supplication with thanksgiving let your requests be made known to God. And the peace of God, which surpasses all understanding, will guard your hearts and your minds in Christ Jesus.
Philippians 4:6-7

Gladys would have been very familiar with these verses from Philippians, for she relied on it often to give her encouragement during the difficult times. But there were times when Gladys forgot that verse. After such a long hike through the mountains with all those children, she was tired and unwell, and when there appeared to be no way across the Yellow River she became very anxious. That happens to all of us at sometime or other. We look around at what is not going right for us and begin to worry. And that's why God had the apostle Paul write these verses to the Philippian church. They needed to be reminded that instead of worrying, they should pray. God wants to hear our requests, our worries and our concerns. He's the one who can take care of them. And he can take away the worry and give us peace instead.

Gladys Alyward's journey through the mountains took twenty-seven days altogether. God kept them safe from the Japanese soldiers. He gave them strength to finish their long walk, even when they were hungry and tired. Once the children were safely in Sian, Gladys became very ill. She spent several months in a hospital recovering. But God healed her so she was able to once again travel to the mountain villages to share the Gospel of Christ.

‹HINA

FA‹T FIL‹

China is the fourth largest country in the world. Shanghai and Beijing are two of the largest and most populous cities in the world. Beijing is the capital. Tienanmen Square, in Beijing, is the world's largest public gathering place.

Because China is officially the most populated country in the world, the Chinese Government has adopted a 'one child' policy in an effort to curb the high numbers. Unfortunately, this also makes China one of the fastest aging countries.

Mandarin Chinese is listed as the official language. However, there are fifty-five official minorities in China that speak a total of 206 different dialects. The Chinese language has over 20,000 characters. The average Chinese only learns about 5,000 of these in his lifetime.

The Great Wall of China is over 1500 miles in length and is regarded as one of the Seven Wonders of the World.

Map of China in the 1900s

BIBLE CHARACTERS

You have now read four stories about women who lived in history. Even though they lived in different countries and at different times, they all loved God and took risks to serve him. As they studied their Bibles, those women read many stories about Biblical women who also loved God and faced risks. The next two chapters are about a woman who bravely moved to a foreign country and another who calmed an angry man. They chose to obey God, even when it was difficult and dangerous. They are good examples for us too.

RUTH:
THE FOREIGNER

RUTH 1-4

Taking a risk can sometimes mean doing something you haven't done before. It may not be exactly dangerous, but it could make your life very different, even difficult. Moving to a new place, for instance. You have to leave your home, your friends, your school and all the people and places that are familiar to you. Going to a new place means you have to get used to new people and new routines, and that's a risk. What if you don't like the new people? Or worse, what if they don't like you? Instead of feeling happy and secure, you could end up feeling miserable and lonely.

There's a story in the Old Testament about a woman who had to face such a risk. Ruth moved away from the home she had always known to go to a new country. The people there had different ways of doing things, and they didn't always welcome people from other countries. So when Ruth decided to move, she was taking a risk that she might be very unhappy.

Ruth's story is found in the Old Testament, in a short book named for her. Ruth was born in the country of Moab, which was located east of Israel, on the other side of the Dead Sea. When you look at a map today, it's where the country of Jordan is now located. The hilly country and fertile valleys received lots of rain, which meant that the crops grew well. But the people who lived in Moab didn't love God. They worshipped idols, among them an idol called Chemosh. When Ruth was growing up, she saw nothing wrong with that. She was taught to serve idols as if they were real gods. She had never heard about the true and living God.

We aren't told in the Bible how old Ruth was when she met her future husband. All the Bible tells us is that she married one of the sons of Elimelech and Naomi, a family from Israel. Ruth must have surprised her parents by wanting to marry a foreigner, someone who didn't worship their gods. And it's likely her husband's family were not pleased at first either. But God had caused certain events to happen because he had a special plan for Ruth.

Elimelech had moved his family to Moab because of a famine in Israel. He had sold his land in Bethlehem and moved to a place that had good crops and a promise of a better life. While they were living in Moab, Elimelech died, leaving his wife Naomi to raise their two sons, Mahlon and Chilion. When the boys grew up, they wanted to marry, and since they were living in Moab, they chose to marry women who lived nearby.

When Elimelech and Naomi had arrived in Moab, they must have been treated with some suspicion. The Moabites feared Israel because the Israelites, with God's help, had defeated and driven out the neighbouring Canaanites. And the Israelites only worshipped one God who couldn't be seen, not idols made of precious gold and silver or carved out of beautiful stone or wood.

We are not told how Ruth met her husband or how it was decided they should marry. But what we do know is that Elimelech's family had continued to worship the true and living God, even when they lived in a foreign country. We know this because when Ruth came to live in their home, she learned about God.

Back then the custom was for the wife to live with her husband's family after they were married. Ruth could still visit her own family, but she no longer belonged to them. Instead she was expected to live not just with her husband, but also with her mother-in-law, Naomi, and even her husband's brother and sister-in-law, Orpah. She was also expected to worship as her husband did. God used this custom to make sure that Ruth had an opportunity to learn about the true and living God.

For ten years they all lived happily together as a family. Then something dreadful happened. Both Mahlon and Chilion died. Now Naomi, Ruth and Orpah were all widows. In Old Testament times women didn't work at jobs outside their homes. The men in the family supported the women and children by working in the fields or as merchants or traders. When there were no men left in the family, the women had no way to buy food or clothing. And even worse, because Naomi's relatives lived back in Israel, they couldn't help the women either. They became poor very quickly.

But then Naomi heard some good news. The Bible says:

> '...she had heard in the fields of Moab that the
> LORD had visited his people and given them food.'
> [Ruth 1:6b]

The famine in Israel was over and Naomi wanted to go home. So she called her daughters-in-law together and told them of her plan. Both Ruth and Orpah wanted to go with her because they loved Naomi. So they started out on the long journey. But then Naomi had second thoughts about Ruth and Orpah coming to live in Israel. Was it really a good idea? So she said,

> 'Go, return each of you to her mother's house. May the LORD deal kindly with you, as you have dealt with the dead and with me. The LORD grant that you may find rest, each of you in the house of her husband!' Then she kissed them, and they lifted up their voices and wept. And they said to her, 'No, we will return with you to your people.' [Ruth 1:8-10]

At first both women promised to stay with Naomi because they loved her. The very idea of leaving her made them all cry. But then Orpah began to have doubts as Naomi reminded them how difficult it would be for them in Israel. Naomi couldn't give them any hope of getting another husband. Naomi was returning to her home, but she had nothing to offer them there. Naomi thought it would be best for them to return to their mothers, who would find new husbands to care for them.

Ruth must have thought carefully about what she should do. If she went back home to Moab she was still young enough to remarry and have children. But it would also mean she would have to return to worshipping idols.

On the other hand, if she stayed with Naomi and went with her to Bethlehem, she would still be very poor. And she would be a foreigner in a strange country. She knew, as Naomi did, that she was unlikely to find another Israelite man to marry her because she came from an idol-worshipping country. God had told his people not to marry anyone who came from such countries.

Orpah thought about these things too, and decided she didn't want to take the risk of leaving Moab. So she kissed Naomi goodbye and left. But Ruth decided to take the risk. The Bible tells us 'Ruth clung to her'. [Ruth 1:14b].

Still Naomi tried to persuade her to follow Orpah back to Moab.

> 'See, your sister-in-law has gone back to her
> people and to her gods; return after your sister-
> in-law.' [Ruth 1:15]

Can you imagine the scene on the road that led back into Israel? Travellers moving past them must have wondered what these women were discussing so intently as they sometimes cried and hugged each other. Then one woman finally left, kissing the others goodbye, and walked back down the road that led to Moab. The other two, one older, one younger stood together in a tight embrace. If people had stopped to listen, they would have heard Ruth's reply to Naomi.

> 'Do not urge me to leave you or to return from
> following you. For where you go I will go, and

where you lodge I will lodge. Your people shall
be my people, and your God my God. Where
you die I will die, and there will I be buried. May
the LORD do so to me and more also if anything
but death parts me from you.' [Ruth 1:16-17]

With her promise, Ruth showed Naomi that following
God was more important to her than a comfortable
home, lots of food or a husband to take care of her. She
loved her mother-in-law too and didn't want to leave
her alone with no one to care for her. How glad Naomi
must have felt. Even though she was returning home
a widow, with no money and her sons dead, she had
Ruth who loved her. And more important they both
loved God.

Life in Bethlehem wasn't easy for Ruth and Naomi.
Naomi's friends welcomed her back but they had little
to share with her. So Ruth and Naomi did the only thing
that poor people could do at that time. Ruth went to the
fields of the wealthy landowners where the crops were
being harvested.

It was a happy time for the landowners because the
crops had grown very well. The reapers cut down the
barley and wheat and gathered it into bundles. Once the
crops were gathered the poor people were allowed to
come into the fields and gather up any bits of the crops
that had been left behind. This was called gleaning and
God had commanded that landowners do this so that no
one in Israel would starve.

Ruth became a gleaner. It was back-breaking work. She had to walk bent over, looking carefully around for any sheaves of wheat or barley that had fallen out of the reapers' bundles. She would put the crops she found in a cloth bag that she carried over her shoulder. She hoped to fill the bag and then take it home to grind it into flour and meal and make it into bread. But just imagine how many fields she would have to glean if the reapers were very careful not to let much fall out of their bundles! Some days she might only find a little.

Then one day Ruth found herself in a field owned by a man named Boaz. After asking the overseer's permission, Ruth joined the other gleaners and worked all morning. While she was working, Boaz himself arrived at the field to see how his reapers were getting on. Imagine Ruth's surprise when Boaz came up to her in the field. Their conversation is reported in the Bible.

> Then Boaz said to Ruth, 'Now, listen, my daughter, do not go to glean in another field or leave this one, but keep close to my young women. Let your eyes be on the field that they are reaping, and go after them. Have I not charged the young men not to touch you? And when you are thirsty, go to the vessels and drink what the young men have drawn.' Then she fell on her face, bowing to the ground, and said to him, 'Why have I found favour in your eyes, that you should take notice of me, since I am

a foreigner?' But Boaz answered her, 'All that
you have done for your mother-in-law since the
death of your husband has been fully told to me,
and how you left your father and mother and
your native land and came to a people that you
did not know before.' [Ruth 2:8-11]

Ruth was overwhelmed with Boaz's kindness. And
Boaz was impressed that Ruth took the risk of leaving
her home country and her family and coming to a place
she had never been before. He knew Ruth worshipped
the true God, even though she had come from an idol-
worshipping country, so he asked God to reward Ruth
for that. Boaz gave her a blessing.

'The LORD repay you for what you have done,
and a full reward be given you by the LORD, the
God of Israel, under whose wings you have come
to take refuge!' [Ruth 2:12]

Ruth replied humbly, realizing just how much kindness
Boaz was showing her.

'I have found favour in your eyes, my lord,
for you have comforted me and spoken kindly
to your servant, though I am not one of your
servants.' [Ruth 2:13]

Boaz's kindness didn't stop there. At the mid-day meal,
Boaz invited her to help herself to the food he had
provided for his workers. Then he instructed his reapers
to deliberately let many of the stalks of grain fall out

of their bundles so that Ruth had lots of stalks to glean that afternoon. By the end of the day she had almost a whole bushel of grain to take home to Naomi.

Just imagine how amazed Naomi was when Ruth arrived home for supper bringing all that food with her. She started asking questions right away.

> 'Where did you glean today? And where have you worked? Blessed be the man who took notice of you.' [Ruth 2:19]

So Ruth told Naomi all about her day. Naomi was very pleased to hear how kind Boaz had been to her daughter-in-law. She told Ruth that Boaz was a distant relative of hers. They thanked the Lord that Ruth now had a safe and plentiful place to glean.

Ruth had taken the risk to come to Israel with Naomi, not expecting anything other than poverty and Naomi's love. However, God does promise us blessing if we follow him and obey him even when it's difficult. God already had a plan in place for Ruth.

Naomi explained to Ruth that Boaz was a kinsman-redeemer. We don't have anything like that in our families today. But back in Bible times God had told the Israelites that they should care for their family members in a particular way, even those who were distantly related. If anyone in their family became poor and had to sell their land, a wealthy member of the family must buy it back for them. Also, if a woman's husband died, then someone in her husband's extended family should marry the widow so she would have someone to provide for her. These were the duties of a kinsman-redeemer.

So Naomi instructed Ruth to approach Boaz and ask him if he would become their kinsman-redeemer; would he buy back or redeem the land Elimelech had sold all those years ago and marry Ruth? Boaz was more than willing to do it all. He was a wealthy man, and he greatly admired Ruth for her steadfast love for God and Naomi. Boaz worked out the details with the city elders and then married Ruth. He took care of Naomi too. And when Ruth and Boaz had their first child, he became Naomi's grandchild too.

God honoured Ruth for her risk-taking. He gave Ruth a new family which led to her becoming part of an even greater plan that God had in mind. Ruth, a foreigner, became part of the family tree of King David and the Lord Jesus.

ABIGAIL:
THE WOMAN WHO CALMED AN ANGRY MAN

1 SAMUEL 25

Abigail had married a very wealthy man. She had a big house and lots of servants. Her husband owned 3,000 sheep and 1,000 goats, and lots of land. Abigail should have had a happy home, because she had all those good things. But, no, she didn't. Her husband, Nabal, was not a nice man. All his wealth had only made him greedy and unable to share with others. He spoke harshly to people, insulting and belittling them. He was quick-tempered and most unpleasant to work for. Abigail's home life was not easy at all. But Abigail wanted to be a good wife, even if her husband was difficult. So she went about her job of caring for her home with a quiet and meek spirit. While her life was not all she may have wanted it to be, she must have assumed that this was what God had planned for her. Certainly, she wouldn't have to take any risks for God as the wife of a wealthy man, would she?

Abigail lived in Israel during the time of King Saul. Israel was at peace with its neighbours but was not so peaceful inside. King Saul had rejected God and God had chosen David to be the next king when Saul died. Saul was angry and tried to kill David to stop God's plan. David had to go into hiding and many men came to join him because they no longer respected Saul as their king. The country of Israel became divided, some supporting Saul and some supporting David.

Abigail, however, had other things on her mind. The work that occupied her when our story begins was a huge feast. It was spring and time to shear the sheep of their warm winter coats. All the shepherds working for Nabal gathered the sheep together and spent a number of days shearing all those 3,000 sheep. At the end of the shearing Nabal always held a feast to celebrate the harvest of wool and all the workers were invited. Nabal loved a good party and always ate and drank more than anyone else. It was

Abigail's job to see that enough food was prepared for everyone to enjoy, and enough places for them all to sit at the tables. But something happened to interrupt the harvest party that year.

The first that Abigail heard about it was when one of the shepherds came rushing into the house to find her. He quickly told her the whole story. David and his men had been camped all winter in the mountains near where Nabal's shepherds cared for the sheep. David's men had been good to the shepherds, helping them especially by killing any wild animals who threatened the flocks and protecting them from thieves. The shepherds said that

> '...the men were very good to us, and we suffered no harm, and we did not miss anything when we were in the fields, as long as we went with them. They were a wall to us both by night and by day, all the while we were with them keeping the sheep.'
> [I Samuel 25:15-16]

Now that the shearing feast had begun, David had sent messengers to greet Nabal, asking for some sort of thank you gift. But Nabal had shouted at them:

> 'Who is David? Who is the son of Jesse? There are many servants these days who are breaking away from their masters. Shall I take my bread and my water and my meat that

> I have killed for my shearers and give it to
> men who come from I do not know where?'
> [1 Samuel 25:10-11]

David and his men became very angry with Nabal and now threatened his whole household. The shepherd had come to warn Abigail.

> 'Now therefore know this and consider what
> you should do, for harm is determined against
> our master and against all his house, and he is
> such a worthless man that one cannot speak
> to him.' [1 Samuel 25:17]

Just imagine how startled Abigail was! Here she had worked hard to have the feast ready, hoping everything would go well. But instead of the party beginning, she was told her whole household was in danger of being killed. And the man who was threatening them was none other than David, God's choice for the next king of Israel. Suddenly Abigail's life had become very dangerous and she had to do something about it.

Abigail didn't have much time to think. She had to make a choice quickly. She knew her husband was a nasty man. If he had been rude to a warrior like David then he deserved to be treated badly, especially when David and his men had been so helpful to Nabal's shepherds. Abigail could have decided to run away and hide, hoping to be safe when David and his men arrived at her home. But she didn't. She chose instead to take a risk, to see if she couldn't be a peacemaker between her husband and David.

Knowing that all David had asked for was some reward for his help, Abigail decided to give him that. She knew that his men had no way of getting food unless someone gave it to them. And here was her kitchen full to bursting with all the food prepared for the feast. So she gave the orders to her servants to pack up some of it:

> ...two hundred loaves and two skins of wine and five sheep already prepared and five seahs of parched grain and a hundred clusters of raisins and two hundred cakes of figs...
> [1 Samuel 25:18]

That was a lot of food to load up on the donkeys, but she knew she had four hundred men to feed. Then she sent a servant on ahead to meet David and ask him to wait for her.

Can you imagine how Abigail felt as she climbed onto her donkey to begin her ride out to the mountains where David and his men were living? She didn't even take time to tell her husband where she was going or why. All she could think about was stopping David from doing this terrible thing. Her heart must have been pounding as her donkey climbed through the rocky trails. She must have kept

looking back, making sure her servants and their donkeys carrying the food were keeping close behind her. She also must have rehearsed what she would say when she met David. Then all of a sudden as she came around a bend in the trail she could see David and his men marching down the mountainside toward her.

The Bible tells us a couple of things about Abigail that most people noticed about her right away. She was very beautiful to look at, and she was also beautiful inside. She was a wise woman, known for her discernment or understanding in difficult situations. That was why the shepherd had come to tell her about the problem instead of Nabal. So Abigail wisely did and said a number of things when David and his men stopped in front of her on that mountain pathway.

First, she treated David as if he were already a king. She bowed down to him, showing him the respect her husband should have shown. Then she spoke to David. She had a number of things she knew she needed to say, and some of it was going to take great courage.

Abigail began her speech by apologising for her husband and explaining that she knew nothing of the events until someone told her.

'On me alone, my lord, be the guilt. Please let your servant speak in your ears, and hear

the words of your servant. Let not my lord
regard this worthless fellow, Nabal, for as his
name is, so is he. Nabal[2] is his name, and folly
is with him. But I your servant did not see
the young men of my lord, whom you sent.'
[1 Samuel 25:24-25]

Then she offered him the food she had brought with
her, asking him to give it to his men. Abigail was doing
her best to calm down angry David and his men.

Now came the dangerous part. Abigail knew food
alone wouldn't stop David from going after her
foolish husband. The lack of a reward for protecting
the shepherds and sheep wasn't the real problem. The
real problem was what Nabal had said about David.
Nabal had called David a worthless servant who had
run away from his master King Saul. Nabal had
refused to recognize David as God's choice as the next
king. And that had made David angry, especially
when he had been careful to only stay out of King
Saul's way rather than lead a rebellion against him.
So now Abigail had to remind David of God's plan.
She must have taken a very deep breath before she
began. Telling an angry man something he might not
want to hear was risky. David had already declared
he would kill Nabal. In his anger would he kill her
right there?

---

[2] Nabal means 'foolish'.

She began carefully, telling David she knew he was God's servant and God would protect him from his enemies.

> 'Please forgive the trespass of your servant. For the LORD will certainly make my lord a sure house, because my lord is fighting the battles of the LORD, and evil shall not be found in you so long as you live. If men rise up to pursue you and to seek your life, the life of my lord shall be bound in the bundle of the living in the care of the LORD your God. And the lives of your enemies he shall sling out as from the hollow of a sling.' [1 Samuel 25:28-29]

But then she had to remind him that he had to be careful. While he was waiting for God to make him king of Israel, he had to remember to obey all of God's laws. Killing Nabal would be committing murder. Did he want to be known as the king who killed people who were rude to him? This is what she said:

> 'And when the LORD has done to my lord according to all the good that he has spoken concerning you and has appointed you prince over Israel, my lord shall have no cause of grief or pangs of conscience for having shed blood without cause or for my lord taking vengeance himself. And when the LORD has

dealt well with my lord, then remember your
servant.' [1 Samuel 25:30-31]

Abigail must have held her breath after she finished.
How would David react to being told he should watch
his actions?

There is a verse in Proverbs that says,

Listen to advice and accept instruction,
that you may gain wisdom in the future.
[Proverbs 19:20]

And that's what David did. He listened to the wise
advice that Abigail gave him and accepted her
instruction on how he should behave. He said to her,

'Blessed be the LORD, the God of Israel, who
sent you this day to meet me! Blessed be your
discretion, and blessed be you, who have
kept me this day from bloodguilt and from
avenging myself with my own hand! For as
surely as the LORD, the God of Israel, lives, who
has restrained me from hurting you, unless
you had hurried and come to meet me, truly
by morning there had not been left to Nabal so
much as one male.' [1 Samuel 25:32-34]

David recognized his anger was wrong and he was
grateful for Abigail's courage to tell him so. She had
stopped him from killing Nabal, something he would
have regretted for the rest of his life. Abigail must

have been very relieved to hear David speak those words. She gladly gave the order to her servants to give all the food she had brought to David's men. And as she bowed once more to him, David said,

> 'Go up in peace to your house. See, I have obeyed your voice, and I have granted your petition.' [1 Samuel 25:35]

Abigail did as David said, and returned to her house. God had blessed her wise actions and her husband and household were safe. But now she had one more task. She had to tell her husband Nabal what had happened. She must have returned home feeling worried about how he would respond. Nabal was not a wise man like David.

To her great surprise she found everyone feasting as if there had been no threat and there was Nabal, behaving as if he were a king. When she came up to him she realized he was very drunk, so she went away to her room. She would wait until morning, when he was sober, to tell him all that had happened.

The next morning Abigail wasted no time. She found Nabal and told him the entire story, especially of how close to death he and the entire household had come. But she assured him that David was no longer angry and he would spare them. When Nabal heard the news he was so shocked that he had a stroke. Suddenly he couldn't move or talk. His servants rushed in to carry him to his bed, but there was nothing anyone could do for him. After ten days Nabal died.

When David heard what had happened he knew that God had used Abigail to prevent him from doing wrong. She had given him good advice. She was just the kind of woman he wanted to have as his wife. So he sent a messenger to her, asking her to marry him. Abigail said yes. She saw that David was a good man to have for a husband. He loved God and wanted to obey his commands. So she saddled up her donkey, took five women from her household with her and went with the messenger to meet her new husband.

Abigail took a risk to bring good advice to an angry man and God blessed her courage. Do you have that courage? This doesn't mean that we should go around being 'know-it-alls' telling people every time we see them doing wrong. Remember how Abigail spoke to David, with respect and meekness. How we speak is just as important as what we say. Always 'season your words with salt' as it says in Colossians 4:6, speaking with kindness just as you would want someone to speak to you.

Map of Israel and Moab

WHAT NEXT?

So, after reading all those stories, could you be a risk taker too? Have you got what it takes to serve God with courage? Could you choose to be exiled for doing the right thing? Could you risk telling someone very important that they ought to serve God? Could you go on a dangerous journey and risk death or prison to tell others of God's love?

God might not ask you to do such dangerous things, but he does ask everyone who is a Christian to be willing to serve him no matter what. Could you risk losing friends because you chose to obey God's law instead of doing some mischief with those friends? Do you have the courage to say to God, 'I will serve you no matter where you want me to go or what you want me to do'? God is looking for us to have willing hearts to serve him even when it is difficult. And in the end, he has promised us great reward.

WHO IS LINDA FINLAYSON?

Linda Finlayson writes the adventure stories of real people, bringing together her love of books, children and history. She has enjoyed working with children in schools, churches and children's clubs. Linda is a Canadian living in the suburbs of Philadelphia in the USA. She is married and has one son.

Linda has also written *Wilfred Grenfell: Arctic Adventurer* and three other books in the Risktakers series:

Strength and Devotion
Adventure and Faith
Danger and Dedication

RISKTAKER QUIZ

Elizabeth Welch

1. Where had Elizabeth's husband been imprisoned?

2. Where in Europe had Elizabeth and her family been exiled?

3. Who was Elizabeth's father?

4. What did Elizabeth need in order to seek permission from the king for her husband to return to Scotland?

5. Why did Elizabeth not accept the king's one condition?

RISKTAKER QUIZ

Mary Slessor

1. What did Mary promise God she would do with her life when she became a Christian?

2. Why were some children abandoned by the Okoyong people?

3. Why had warriors captured a dozen people from Chief Akpo's village?

4. What did Chief Edem eventually do instead of killing the prisoners?

5. Mary spoke to the whole village about God's sacrifice for us. What was that sacrifice?

RISKTAKER QUIZ

Mildred Cable

1. Which missionary organisation did Mildred serve with?

2. What was Mildred's occupation?

3. Who were Mildred's fellow missionaries?

4. What did Mildred say to the General about his soul?

5. After leaving the city where did Mildred, her friends and daughter travel to?

RISKTAKER QUIZ

Gladys Aylward

1. How did Gladys travel to China and what did she have with her?

2. Why were the Japanese angry? Why did they want Gladys captured?

3. When Gladys gathered the children together, what did they do the evening before setting off for Sian?

4. What did Gladys do to encourage the children on their long walk?

5. How did God answer the prayer of Gladys and the children for a way across the river?

RISKTAKER QUIZ

Ruth

1. In which country was Ruth born?

2. According to custom, which relatives was Ruth expected to live with?

3. What did Ruth and Naomi do in order to find food?

4. What did Naomi instruct Ruth to ask Boaz to become?

5. Which family tree did Ruth become a part of when she married Boaz?

RISKTAKER QUIZ

Abigail

1. Who did Abigail marry and what was he like?

2. List the food Abigail arranged to have loaded onto donkeys for David and his men.

3. What did Abigail say and do when she met David?

4. What did Abigail risk doing?

5. What happened to her husband when she told him what she had done?

RISKTAKER QUIZ
ANSWERS

E;IZABETH WELCH

1. Blackness Castle, near Edinburgh.
2. France.
3. John Knox.
4. Courage.
5. The Bible said nothing about having bishops in church, and bishops did as the king told them.

MARY SLESSOR

1. She would become a missionary to Africa.
2. They thought twins were evil and left them to die when they were born.
3. They were to be killed for the death of the Chief's son.
4. He killed a cow.
5. God has sacrificed his own Son to pay the penalty for our sin.

MILDRED CABLE

1. China Inland Mission.
2. Chemist/Nurse.
3. Eva and Francesca French.
4. He needed healing for his soul.
5. Other villages, Moscow and back to England.

GLADYS AYLWARD

1. By train with one suitcase and £2 9p in her pocket.
2. She had told the Chinese where the Japanese troops were hiding.
3. They worshipped God, and had a meal.
4. She sang hymns to God and the children joined in.
5. A Chinese soldier heard their singing and eventually arranged to bring some boats for them.

RUTH

1. Moab.
2. Her husband, mother-in-law, and her husband's brother and sister-in-law.
3. They gleaned in the fields.
4. A Kinsman-redeemer.
5. The family tree of King David and the Lord Jesus.

ABIGAIL

1. Nabal who wasn't a very nice man.
2. Loaves, wine, prepared sheep, grain, raisins and cakes of figs.
3. She treated David as if he were already king. She apologised for the way her husband had responded to him and gave him food for his men.
4. She risked telling an angry man something he might not want to hear.
5. He had a stroke and died.

GLOSSARY

Besiege: to surround a city with an army.

Brazier: a metal pan for holding burning coals.

Breeches: Man's clothing covering from the waist down, usually to the knee (what we would call trousers today).

Carter: someone who drives a cart and cares for the animals.

Chemise: a loose shirt-like undergarment.

Dais: a raised platform.

Doublet: A man's snug-fitting buttoned jacket.

Exile: when someone is forced to leave their home country and cannot return.

Huguenots: members of the Reformed Protestant Church of France.

Jute: a type of plant fibre used to make common items such as rope, twine, chair coverings, curtains, sacks, etc.

King James VI became known as James 1 when he became king of both England and Scotland.

Magic lantern show: An old name for a slideshow, using an early form of slide projector that could achieve simple animation by moving and merging images.

Mandarin: a government official in China.

Millet: a poor quality cereal prepared from the seeds of the millet plant (a tall grass).

Nabal means 'foolish'.

Opium: A bitter, addictive drug.

Paralysis: loss of ability to move a body part.

Plaid: a countryman's cape made of wool.

Presence Chamber: the room the king or queen received ambassadors and petitioners.

Reaper: someone who cuts and gathers crops when they are ripe.

Spigot: A wooden tap fitted to a cask.

CHRISTIAN FOCUS PUBLICATIONS

Christian Christian CF4K Mentor
Focus Heritage

Christian Focus Publications publishes books for adults and children under its four main imprints: Christian Focus, Christian Heritage, CF4K and Mentor. Our books reflect that God's word is reliable and Jesus is the way to know him, and live for ever with him.

Our children's publication list includes a Sunday school curriculum that covers pre-school to early teens; puzzle and activity books. We also publish personal and family devotional titles, biographies and inspirational stories that children will love.

If you are looking for quality Bible teaching for children then we have an excellent range of Bible story and age specific theological books. From pre-school to teenage fiction, we have it covered!

Find us at our web page:
www.christianfocus.com

CF4·K
Because you're never
too young to know Jesus